GROW TOTALLY WEIRD GARDEN

BY JOANNA PONCAVAGE
ILLUSTRATED BY PETER GEORGESON

Andrews and McMeel
A Universal Press Syndicate Company
Kansas City

This book is dedicated to every big person who shows a little person how to plant a seed.

Grow a Totally Weird Garden text copyright © 1996 by Joanna Poncavage. Produced by becker&mayer!, Ltd. All rights reserved. Printed in Canada. No part of this book may be used or reproduced in any manner whatsoever without permission except in the context of reviews.

Design by Leandra Jones

For information, write:
Andrews and McMeel, a Universal Press Syndicate Company,
4900 Main Street, Kansas City, Missouri 64112.

ISBN: 0-8362-1082-4

Grow a Totally Weird Garden is a packaged set produced by becker&mayer!, Ltd, which includes six packets of seed, peat pellets, and this book.

Other children's kits from becker&mayer!:

Amazing Airplanes Book & Kit
The Amazing Sandcastle Builder's Kit
Build Your Own Dinosaurs
Build Your Own Bugs
Fun with Ballet
Fun with Ballet: Sleeping Beauty
Fun with Electronics
Fun with Electronics, Jr.
The Ant Book & See-Through Model
The Bat Book & See-Through Model

CONTENTS

WHERE DO GARDENS COME FROM?

They come from seeds like the ones in the packets that came with this book!

You hold in your hand the beginning of a great adventure! When you put these little seeds in the ground, they will come alive and start to grow. Some will become plants that are good to eat. Some will become plants that are more fun than your goldfish. But all of these seeds will grow up to be plants that are weird and wacky:

- giant pumpkins bigger than your little sister
- carrots shaped like Ping-Pong balls
- tiny red tomatoes you can eat in one bite
- sunflowers as big as trees
- purple beans that turn green when you cook them
- a plant that folds up its leaves when you touch it.

Just follow the instructions in this book, and you'll soon have a very amazing garden!

WHAT IS A SEED?

A seed is like a little suitcase that contains everything a baby plant needs to begin a new life.

The hard shell of the seed protects the seed before it finds a good place to grow. That's where gardeners come in—they put the little seed somewhere safe and warm and wet so it can begin its new life.

A seed soaks up water like a sponge. Water softens up the hard shell and wakes up the little plant inside. Then the plant begins to grow, just like a baby bird grows inside an egg. When the baby bird is strong enough, it breaks the eggshell with its beak. A plant breaks its shell too.

When a plant wakes up and breaks through its shell, its root begins to grow down. The leaves of the plant begin to grow up. Soon you will see something tiny and green poking its nose up through the dirt. In a few more days, little leaves are reaching up to the sky and getting bigger.

WHAT IS A PLANT?

A plant is alive, just like you and your little sister and your pet goldfish. Plants and people and animals are made up of many (trillions, in fact) tiny parts called "cells." Each cell has a different job to do to keep us alive.

A leaf is a plant's food factory. A leaf is green because its cells contain something called "chlorophyll." Chlorophyll helps the cells of the leaf mix sunlight, water, and air to make food for the plant. It's like magic! This transformation of energy and elements into something the plant can use to grow bigger is called "photosynthesis."

Plants feed themselves. Animals eat plants. People eat plants. Plants feed the world.

WHAT IS A ROOT?

A root grows down into the ground and holds the plant in one place so it won't blow away in the wind. A root collects water and minerals from the soil. Minerals are kind of like vitamins for plants. They help plants grow strong and healthy.

WHAT IS A FLOWER?

Flowers, the pretty blossoms on plants, are bright and colorful because it is their job to attract bees and other insects to plants to help with the important task of making seeds.

Way down deep inside the flowers is a drop of a sweet liquid called "nectar." A bee visits a flower to collect a sip of this nectar, which it will take back to its hive to make honey.

But while the bee is inside the flower, it is bumbling around and knocking a yellow powder called "pollen" from one part of the flower, called a "stamen," onto another part of the flower, called a "pistil." The pistil needs the pollen to make seeds that will grow into new plants. This cooperation between bees and flowers is called "pollination," or "fertilization." The seeds in the little packets that came with this book were made with the help of bees.

WHAT IS DIRT?

"Soil" is what we call the top layer of stuff that makes up the
planet Earth. Sometimes we call it "ground" or "dirt."
This is what is in it:

ANIMAL THINGS

- Bugs
- Worms
- Spiders
- Bacteria

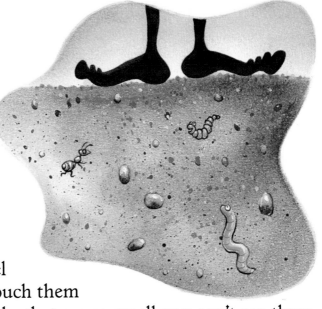

MINERAL THINGS

- Big rocks
- Medium rocks
- Little rocks
- Teeny tiny rocks
  so small they feel
  soft when you touch them
- Teenier tinier rocks that are so small you can't see them

PLANT THINGS

- Fungi
- Molds
- Plant roots
  Plant roots collect little pieces of all of these things found in
  the soil. Roots bring these things inside the plant so the plant
  can use them to grow bigger.

THE FIRST GARDEN

A long time ago, before people had letters to write words or wheels to roll wagons or chocolate to make chocolate cake, there were no gardens, either. People ate the plants that grew wild everywhere. In those days, people spent a lot of time walking around and looking for special plants that tasted good. They picked fruits and nuts from trees and bushes. They dug up roots that grew underground. They collected grains from grass plants.

Then one day (about 10,000 years ago, to be precise), somebody noticed that plants grow from seeds. They decided to plant the seeds of their favorite foods close to home so they wouldn't need to spend so much time hunting for their supper.

It was the first garden on earth.

THE BIG, THE LITTLE,
AND THE PURPLE

These are the plants that will grow from the seeds that came with this book.

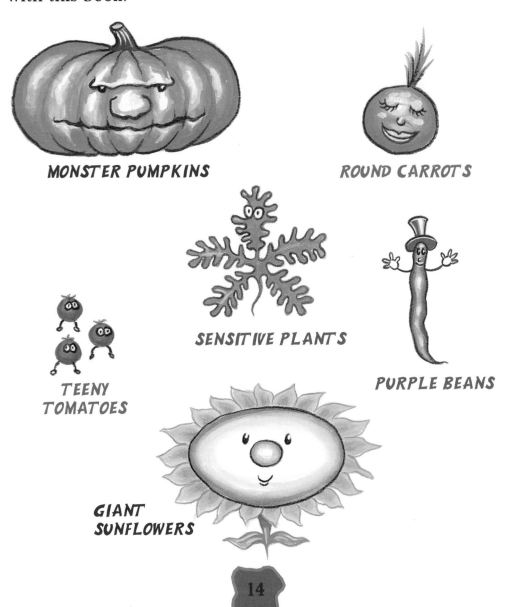

MONSTER PUMPKINS

ROUND CARROTS

SENSITIVE PLANTS

TEENY
TOMATOES

PURPLE BEANS

GIANT
SUNFLOWERS

BIG MOON PUMPKINS

These orange monsters can grow to weigh 200 pounds. (If you weigh 50 pounds, that's four times as big as you are!) If your pumpkin gets that big, you can enter it in a Giant Pumpkin Contest. The winner of the 1993 World Pumpkin Contest weighed 884 pounds!

HOW A PUMPKIN GROWS

Pumpkins grow on long, stringy plants called vines. Pumpkins need lots and lots of room to grow. Pumpkin vines get so big and healthy, they can cover a car if it's parked in the driveway a little too long. Plant them on the edge of your garden and gently train the vines to grow across the lawn, up a fence, or over the doghouse. Pumpkins like to drink lots and lots of water too.

Later this summer, you will find big yellow flowers beneath the leaves of the pumpkin vine. If you want big pumpkins, pinch off all but one or two or three flowers. After looking pretty for a day or so, the flowers will start to turn into little green pumpkins. These little green pumpkins will grow and grow and grow into big green pumpkins. At the end of summer, they will start to turn orange.

HOW TO HARVEST PUMPKINS

When the pumpkin is bright, bright orange, ask a grown-up to cut the stem a few inches back from where it connects to the pumpkin. Then ask the grown-up to move your big pumpkin to a spot where it won't get too cold at night. (Your front porch is a good place.)

WHAT TO DO WITH A PUMPKIN

Pumpkins are very useful at Halloween for carving faces to keep ghosts away from your house. They also come in handy when your fairy godmother needs something to turn into a coach to take you to the

ball at the prince's palace. You can eat pumpkins, too. Ask a grown-up to help you make a pumpkin pie, or to help you make snacks by roasting the pumpkin seeds you will find inside if you cut the pumpkin open to make a jack-o'-lantern.

Odd Pumpkin Fact

While pumpkins grew wild in the New World, the pilgrims and colonists from the Old World had never seen them before. Around the time of the first Thanksgiving, Native Americans gave lots of pumpkins to the colonists so they wouldn't starve during the winter.

17

THUMBELINA CARROTS

Most carrots are long and orange, like the kind that Bugs Bunny chomps on. Thumbelina carrots are little and round. They look like orange Ping-Pong balls.

HOW A CARROT GROWS

The orange part of the carrot that you eat grows underground. Aboveground, carrots have pretty, ferny leaves that grow straight up and are very well behaved, compared to pumpkins. Keep checking the spot where the green leaves of the carrot top come out of the soil. This is where you will soon see a little orange lump begin to grow. Carrots are delicate plants that don't like to grow next to weeds. Be sure to pull out the weeds that come up around your carrots.

HOW TO HARVEST CARROTS

When the orange part of the carrot is about 1 inch across, it will be very sweet and juicy and crunchy. To bring one up, grasp firmly by the leafy green top close to the ground and pull.

A little one-on-one?

WHAT TO DO WITH A CARROT

You can eat a carrot right after you pull it from the ground, but be sure to wash it very carefully before you eat it. Carrots are very, very good for you. They contain lots of vitamins. Carrots are good in salads. Carrots also make a nice orange soup.

Odd Carrot Fact

A long time ago, carrots escaped from gardens and began to grow on their own wherever they felt like growing. Some people call these wild plants weeds; some people call them wildflowers, because they have frilly white flowers. Another name for these wild carrots is Queen Anne's lace.

19

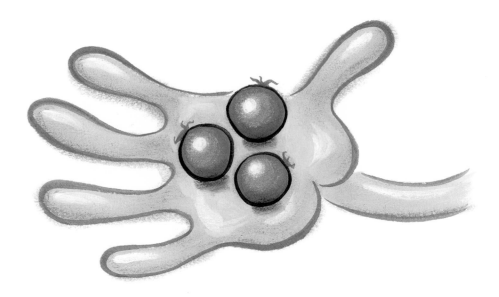

These little tomatoes are as sweet as candy. One whole Sweetie tomato is only a mouthful. Sweetie tomato plants will grow and grow. They might even grow over the fence and into your neighbor's yard.

HOW A TOMATO GROWS

Ask a grown-up to lend you a couple of tomato cages to put over your tomato plants when they are little. As your tomato plant grows, it will climb up the sides of its cage. Soon you will see pretty little yellow flowers appear on the tomato plant. Soon a little green bump will appear at the bottom of the flower. As it gets larger, this little green lump will start to turn pink and then red.

HOW TO HARVEST A TOMATO

A tomato is ready to pick and eat when it is like a newspaper—red all over! One tomato plant will make lots and lots of tomatoes. Take a basket to the garden to put your red ripe tomatoes in as you pick them.

WHAT TO DO WITH A TOMATO

Ask a grown-up to slice a tomato so you can put it between two pieces of bread with some mayonnaise—that's a tomato sandwich! Tomatoes are good in salads, too, and in tomato soup.

Odd Tomato Fact

Tomatoes grow wild in the jungles of Central and South America. When early colonists took tomatoes back to Europe, everybody was afraid to eat them. They thought they were poisonous because they were too pretty to eat. Now tomatoes are the number one plant that people grow in their gardens.

21

ROYAL BURGUNDY BUSH BEANS

Most string beans are green. That's why another name for them is "green beans." These green beans are purple, but they are exactly the same as green beans in every other way. They taste the same, they grow the same, they even smell the same. But they are a very weird color.

HOW BEANS GROW

Beans grow on little bushes. First the bushes will have little white or purple flowers all over them. If you watch carefully, one day you will see tiny little beans starting to grow from the center of each flower.

HOW TO HARVEST BEANS

When the bean is almost as fat as your finger and a little longer than your hand, it's ready to pick. Gently hold the bean plant with one hand and pull the bean from it with your other hand.

WHAT TO DO WITH BEANS

Beans are useful vegetables. What's three-bean salad without beans?

It's my new look!

Odd Bean Fact

These purple beans will turn green when they are cooked. Ask a grown-up to make some beans for supper. As they are cooking in the pot, ask the grown-up to lift the lid so you can see the beans change color. Be very careful!!! Do not touch the pot yourself!

THE SENSITIVE PLANT

The sensitive plant got its name because it can feel you touch it. If you tickle it, it will fold up its little leaves. The leaves will open again in a few minutes. If you touch them again, they'll fold up again.

HOW TO GROW A SENSITIVE PLANT

The sensitive plant is at home in the tropics where it is hot all year round. If you plant some sensitive plant seeds in a flowerpot, they will live in your bedroom all year long. Put the pot on your brightest windowsill. Put a little flat dish under the pot so the water won't drip out when you sprinkle it on to keep the soil moist.

HOW NOT TO HARVEST A SENSITIVE PLANT

This plant is just for fun. You can't eat it, you can't smell it, and you can't take it for a walk. But you can give it a name. That way you won't have to call it "Hey, You" and it won't be offended.

Clyde, come back here and say hi to the people

Odd Sensitive Plant Fact

The sensitive plant is a legume. That means it's related to plants like peas and beans. These plants have special roots. They can make their own plant food underground, with the help of friendly bacteria. Bacteria are one-celled creatures that live everywhere. If your eyes were microscopes, you would see millions of them all over the place.

MAMMOTH GREY STRIPE SUNFLOWERS

Here's a flower that thinks it's a tree! Mammoth Grey Stripe sunflowers will grow 12 feet tall! (If you are 4 feet tall, that's three times as big as you are!) Birds like to eat sunflower seeds. They fly up to the big round flowers and pull the seeds out with their beaks. Crunch! Yum!

HOW A SUNFLOWER GROWS

Sunflowers are monster flowers. Plant them on the north side of your garden so they don't shade the rest of your plants. Sunflowers will keep getting taller all summer long. Go to your garden in the morning and notice which  way the flower is turned. Go back to your garden in the late afternoon and see if the sunflower face is still turned the same way. It moved???? Yes, that's why they call them sunflowers: Their faces follow the sun.

HOW TO HARVEST SUNFLOWERS

By the end of summer, their heads will be big and heavy and bending down. When the back of the flower is starting to turn brown and the petal edges are starting to turn a little brown and dry, ask a grown-up to cut the big flower off its stem. Put it in a dry place for a couple weeks until the seeds are crunchy.

WHAT TO DO WITH A SUNFLOWER

Sunflowers are very useful plants. Animals and people eat their seeds. When it snows and the birds are hungry, put a sunflower head outside in your yard (the picnic table is a good spot) where the birds can find it. You can eat sunflower seeds too. Push, prod, or pull the sunflower seeds off the sunflower head. Crack the shell with your fingers and take out the smooth, gray little nut that's inside. It tastes a little like a peanut or a pecan or a walnut.

Odd Sunflower Fact

Some Native American tribes use black sunflower seeds to dye their clothes. Some people make paper out of the sunflower stalks. But nobody enjoys sunflowers as much as birds do.

WHEN TO START YOUR GARDEN

Before you plant a garden outdoors, you need to help the seeds start growing indoors. Baby plants are tender and need a lot of care.

SIGNS THAT IT'S TIME TO PLANT SEEDS
•Grown-ups are paging through seed catalogs and talking about tomatoes.
•The grocery store is selling little pots of blooming flowers.
•It's time to play baseball.

INSIDE PLANTING INSTRUCTIONS

To start your weird and wacky garden, you'll need the packets of seeds, the peat pellets, some popsicle sticks, and an empty plastic or Styrofoam egg carton. If you don't have any popsicle sticks, now's your chance to nag a grown-up into buying some double-fudgesicles.

1 Ask a grown-up to cut the lid off the egg carton with scissors.

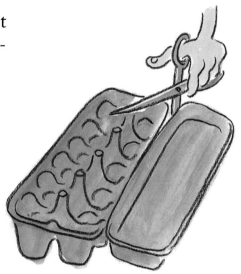

2 Place peat pellets into the empty places in the bottom of the egg carton where the eggs used to be. Place them so the little hole in the middle of the flat peat pellet is facing up.

3 Pour enough water into the egg carton to fill the egg holes halfway up so it surrounds the peat pellets.

4 Wait 30 minutes. The pellets will soak up the water like little sponges and grow plump. If some parts of the pellets are still dry, gently pour a little more water on them.

5 Open the seed packets. Don't tear off the name of what's inside. You might need to know the name of what you're growing later.

6 Shake some seeds out of a packet onto the table. Pick one up and carefully drop it onto the top of the peat pellet. Use the pointed end of a pencil to push the seed gently into the peat pellet so it is snug and cozy. Don't push too far! Just far enough so you can't see it anymore!

Sensitive Plant Alert!

Seeds for sensitive plants need special treatment: First, soak the sensitive plant seeds in warm water for three hours. Then, take them out of the water.

Put one seed at a time onto the top of the peat pellet, but don't push it down into the pellet like you did the other seeds. Just sort of pat the seeds into the peat with your finger. Sensitive plant seeds need to be in the light to sprout into a plant.

7 Write the name of each seed you plant on a pop-sicle stick and stick it in the edge of the peat pellet. This will help you remember which plant is which so you don't put the pumpkins too close to your family's car! (You can buy little wooden plant markers in hardware or plant shops too.)

8 Set the egg carton on a warm, sunny windowsill. The kitchen is a good place. Then you can check on your garden every day at breakfast.

9 Each day, gently pour a little water into the egg carton to keep the peat pellets moist.

10 Some seeds take longer than others to sprout. Here's how long it should take before you see little plants begin to peek out of the peat pellets:

- Pumpkins - 7 days
- Sensitive plant - 3 weeks
- Sunflowers - 10 days
- Beans - 6 days
- Carrots - 14 days
- Tomatoes - 5 days

11 If nothing sprouts, wait a few more days. If you still don't see a little plant starting to grow, push another seed of the same kind into the peat pellet and try again.

OUTSIDE PLANTING INSTRUCTIONS

Your little plants can't stay in that egg carton forever. (Who would be happy calling an egg carton home except an egg, anyway?) Once your plants grow to at least 2 inches tall they'll want to be outside where they can enjoy the sun and the rain. Ask a grown-up to take a walk around your yard with you and help you find a good place for your garden. Look for a spot that will be in the sun most of the day. The soil should be soft and not too rocky. If you don't have a backyard, you can still have a garden. Go to page 50 to see how.

DO NOT PUT YOUR GARDEN HERE!

3 Where you play baseball.

1 Under a tree.

4 Where your dog takes a shortcut into the neighbor's yard.

2 Next to the basketball net.

5 Where a puddle happens every time it rains.

EQUIPMENT

To dig and prepare your garden, you'll need a shovel, a hoe, a rake, and a trowel. (A trowel is a little shovel you can hold in your hand to dig holes.) You'll also need some string. And some more of those popsicle sticks. And a sprinkling can to water your garden later.

PREPARING YOUR GARDEN BED

Ask a grown-up to help you dig your garden. Wait for a day when the ground is not too dry and not too wet. It should be crumbly, and not stick together when you squeeze a handful together.

1 Measure a square about 5 feet long and 5 feet wide. Put a popsicle stick in each corner and connect them with string to mark the sides of the square.

2 Starting along one side, dig into the square with the spade, turning each shovelful upside down. (Careful with those earthworms! They are some of the best friends your garden can have!)

3 Use the hoe to bust up the big chunks of dirt.

4 Use the rake to make the surface of your garden smooth and even.

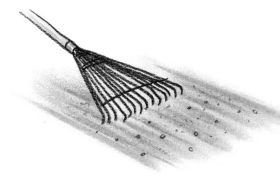

MOVING DAY!

When your little plants are about 2 inches tall, it's time to move them outdoors to your garden.

Special advice:

If you live in a place where it snows in winter, wait until the weather is nice and warm before you move your plants to their new home. Watch what other gardeners in your neighborhood are doing. When they start talking about "putting in some tomatoes," it's time to move your little plants outdoors. (With the exception of that sensitive plant. Wait until nighttime temperatures stay above 55° F—then it's time to move this delicate plant outside.)

Carry the egg carton with your little plants outside to the spot you have prepared. Bring your trowel and a sprinkling can of water too. With the trowel, dig small holes just slightly bigger than the peat pots the baby plants are growing in. Dig the holes far enough apart so that each plant will have lots of room to grow.

This is how much room to give each kind of plant in all directions:

pumpkins - 3 feet

tomatoes - 3 feet

sunflowers - 1 foot

sensitive plant - 1 foot

beans - 5 inches

carrots - 3 inches

Gently set the peat pots into the holes, and fill in around the peat pots with the surrounding soil. Sprinkle the plant with water so the soil around it is wet.

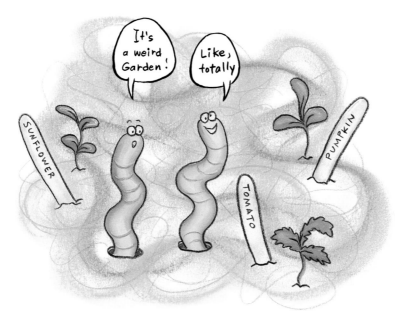

The pumpkins will need lots of room, so put them in the corners where their vines can grow away from the rest of the garden.

The sunflowers need lots of room, to grow UP.

The tomatoes need lots of room, to sprawl, but they will behave if you give them something to climb on. After you plant them in your garden, ask a grown-up to lend you two tomato cages. Tomato cages are made out of wire. Set a cage around each little tomato. The plant will grow up and fill the cage. This will keep the ripe tomatoes out of the dirt later too.

Sensitive plants get sunburned really easily, so put them behind the sunflowers.

THE MAGIC INGREDIENT

Some towns collect leaves, grass clippings, dead plants, tree trimmings and other things people don't want in their backyards anymore. Town employees mix these things together and put them in a pile so they can rot. These unwanted pieces of dead plants then turn into some very valuable stuff called "compost." It contains lots of things living plants need to

grow. If your town makes compost, you might be able to pick some up for free near your town's recycling center. Ask a grown-up. Bring home some compost and spread about 2 inches of it on top of your garden. Mix it into the soil. Your garden will be very happy you did.

Special Garden tip:
Lots of grown-ups have gardens of their own, already dug and smooth. Ask your favorite grown-up if you can borrow a little corner of his or her garden to give your plants a home. Gardeners are very helpful people.

TAKING CARE OF YOUR GARDEN

Gardens enjoy it when you visit them. Move a flat rock, a little wooden bench, or a piece of firewood close to your garden so you have something to sit on while you watch your garden grow. Check on it every day.

HOW TO MULCH YOUR GARDEN

When a grown-up mows the lawn, rake up the cut grass and spread it on the surface of your garden. This is called "mulch." Mulch is like a blanket that keeps the surface of the soil nice and soft so water can soak in. Mulch keeps plant roots cool and happy too. When it rots, mulch changes into stuff that plants need to grow strong and healthy. Plants are like pets, remember? They like to eat too.

HOW TO MAKE COMPOST

Any plant you didn't plant in your garden on purpose is called a "weed." If you like how they look, one or two weeds can stay in your garden. But to give the plants you planted on purpose enough room, pull out the weeds you don't like and put them on a little heap where they can rot. Congratulations! You have just made a compost pile! After the things you put on a compost pile rot and change into something brown and soft and totally unrecognizable, spread the stuff on top of your garden around your plants, just like you did the grass clippings. Compost is a mulch that your plants like to eat. Put any extra grass clippings on your compost pile, too, and mix them in.

HOW TO WATER YOUR GARDEN

Garden plants like to drink lots of water. If your garden hose doesn't reach to your garden, fill a sprinkling can with water and use it to pour water around each plant.

Do this whenever the soil around your garden plants dries out. Do it very gently so the soil around the plants does not wash away. Watering your garden is a good excuse to get muddy.

THE INSTANT GARDEN

What, you might ask, are you going to do with all those seeds that are still in their little packets? You can save them for next year, or give them to friends, so they can grow their own weird and wacky garden.

Or when the weather is warm, you can plant some of them right into the ground outside! Of the seeds that came with this book, carrots, beans, sunflowers, and pumpkins will grow just fine if you plant them right into the garden. The sensitive plant and tomatoes would rather start growing indoors where it's nice and safe and warm.

With your trowel, scratch a little ditch in the surface of the soil. It should be about half an inch deep.

This is how far apart to put each kind of seed in the little ditch:

- Carrots - 1½ inches
- Beans - 3 inches
- Sunflowers - 1 foot
- Pumpkins - 3 feet

THE INDOOR GARDEN

Just because you live in an apartment without a yard doesn't mean you can't have a garden. All you need is some dirt and something to put it in. You can buy dirt for plants in many stores. It is sold in plastic bags marked "potting soil." Sure, you could go outside and dig up some dirt from anywhere, but it will have weed seeds in it and you'll get all kinds of unknown plants sprouting.

Cans that food comes in make good containers for growing vegetables indoors. Ask a grown-up to take off one end of some cans and punch a couple little holes in the other end. Fill the cans with dirt and set them on a dish or tray to keep things neat. Put the can with its dish or tray on your sunniest windowsill. If you have a little patio or porch, that would be a great place too.

Pour water onto the dirt in the cans. Plant seeds into the dirt the same way we told you to plant them in the little peat pellets on page 33. When the seeds sprout, you don't have to move them anywhere! Just keep them watered and make sure those sunflowers have enough headroom. And keep those pumpkin vines from taking over the bathroom.

BUGS

All bugs are fun to watch. But some bugs like to eat your garden plants. These are bad bugs. Good bugs don't want to eat your plants. They want to eat the bad bugs that are eating your plants.

THESE ARE GOOD:

LADYBUGS

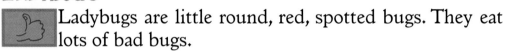 Ladybugs are little round, red, spotted bugs. They eat lots of bad bugs.

LACEWINGS

👍 Lacewings have wings you can see through. They eat lots of bad bugs.

BEES

👍 Bees spread pollen from flower to flower. Flowers like this. Visits from bees help the seeds that are growing inside the flowers grow up to be better plants.

THESE ARE BAD:

TOMATO HORNWORM

One tomato hornworm can eat lots of leaves off your tomato plant. If you find one, ask a grown-up to kick it into the next county.

SNAILS

Snails are not really bugs. They are slimy little things that hide under leaves during the day and come out when the sun isn't shining. Go snail hunting on a cloudy day. Drop any snails you find into a cup of soapy water. When they are dead, pour them onto your compost pile.

MEXICAN BEAN BEETLE

If you find these beetles on your beans, pick them off and drop them into a cup of soapy water. Young Mexican bean beetles are fuzzy and bright yellow. Drop them into soapy water too. Then add them to your compost pile.

EARTHWORMS ARE YOUR FRIENDS

Earthworms live below ground and eat dirt. They eat dirt because they are tunneling through the soil in search of tastier morsels, such as old pieces of dead plants. As this dirt and plant garbage passes through a worm, it comes out the other end filled with good things that living plants need to grow. Earthworms are little fertilizer factories. Earthworms are your gardening assistants. As they tunnel through the ground, they make the soil better by making places for water to run down to where plant roots are. Air comes down the tunnels too. Air and water are very important for keeping plant roots happy.

Earthworms can live for 10 years or more.

If you find a lot of earthworms when you dig around in the dirt, it means the soil is rich and fertile and plants will grow well there. If you uncover a worm, bury it again. Earthworms will die if they get too much sunlight.

MORE WEIRD AND WACKY PLANTS

DEVIL'S CLAW

This plant is a pretty little bush with pink flowers that slowly turn into creepy crawly claws. Native Americans in the Southwest once grew LOTS of these claws. They ate the claw's seeds, and they used the claw's stringy parts to weave baskets. Be careful with these claws— they have sharp points when they are dry.

(Sources: Native Seeds/SEARCH; address follows.)

PEANUTS

Peanuts grow underground inside brown shells. Peanuts are related to peas, beans, and sensitive plants. Peanut flowers send out little tentacles (like an octopus) that dig themselves into the soil under the peanut plant. New peanuts grow underground on the end of these tentacles. If you grow peanuts, elephants might visit your garden.

(Sources: W. Atlee Burpee Co.; Park Seed Co.; addresses follow.)

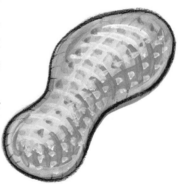

SCARLET RUNNER BEANS

These beans can grow higher than tomato vines and farther than pumpkin vines. If you plant them around a bunch of long sticks tied together at one end and spread apart at the other end, the beans will climb up the sticks and make a bean teepee for you to sit in. Scarlet runner beans have pretty red flowers that hummingbirds like to visit to drink the sweet juice inside.

(Sources: Native Seeds/SEARCH; W. Atlee Burpee Co.— Burpee sells a bean teepee seed package; addresses follow.)

GOURDS

Gourds can be very brightly colored in yellow, orange, green, and stripes! They get hard when they are ripe. They make great musical rattles! If you dry them, their seeds will bounce around inside when you shake them.

(Sources: W. Atlee Burpee Co.; Park Seed Co.; Native Seeds/SEARCH; Thompson & Morgan; addresses follow.)

BIRDHOUSE GOURDS, BASKET GOURDS, AND BOTTLE GOURDS

Before there were stores, people used to make their own bird-houses, baskets, and bottles out of gourds. These gourds grow on big vines that will cover a house if it's in the way. Give the vines lots of room. Some people think these gourds floated across the Atlantic Ocean from Africa to South America a long time ago. The people that lived in the New World needed bird's nests, baskets, and bottles, too, so they started to grow them in their gardens.

(Sources: W. Atlee Burpee Co.; Native Seeds/SEARCH; Thompson & Morgan; addresses follow.)

FUNNY PUMPKINS

"Lumina" is a white pumpkin. Ghosts like it. "Jack Be Little" and "Munchkin" pumpkins are orange and only as big as an apple. "Rouge Vif D'Etampes" is a pretty red pumpkin with a French name. It's the kind of pumpkin Cinderella's fairy godmother turned into a coach.

(Sources: W. Atlee Burpee Co.; Park Seed Co.; addresses follow.)

POPCORN

An ear of popcorn looks like the kind of corn you eat in the summertime. Popcorn kernels can be blue or pink or white or yellow, but it all pops up fluffy and white when you take the kernels off the cob and put them in a popcorn popper.

(Sources: W. Atlee Burpee Co.; Park Seed Co.; addresses follow.)

LIVING STONES

These are desert plants that look like little pebbles. They decided to disguise themselves as pebbles so animals won't eat them. They can live to be 90 years old. They can go for months without water.

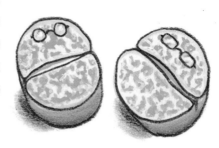

(Sources: Park Seed Co.; Thompson & Morgan; addresses follow.)

WALKING STICK CABBAGE

Most cabbages grow low and close to the ground. Walking stick cabbages grow on stems that can be 5 feet tall. These stems are hard enough for people to use them as canes.

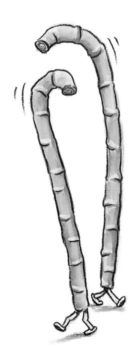

(Sources: Thompson & Morgan; address follows.)

LOOFAH GOURDS

These gourds have bath sponges inside them. Plant them like pumpkins. When they are big, pick the gourds and dry them indoors for a few weeks. Then soak them in water for a day. Then peel off the mushy part. What's left is a fibrous chunk that is good for cleaning things, especially you!

(Sources: W. Atlee Burpee Co.; Park Seed Co.; Thompson & Morgan; addresses follow.)

SOURCES

Write and ask them to send you a catalog.

W. Atlee Burpee Co.
300 Park Ave.
Warminster, PA 18974
(Catalog is free.)

Park Seed Co.
Cokesbury Road
Greenwood, SC 29647
(Catalog is free.)

Native Seeds/SEARCH
2509 N. Campbell Ave. #325
Tucson, AZ 85719
(Send $1 for a catalog.)

Thompson & Morgan
Dept. PRS
Jackson, NJ 08527
(Catalog is free.)